SECURITY OFFICER HANDBOOK

SECURITY OFFICER HANDBOOK

A GUIDE FOR THE ENTRY-LEVEL SECURITY OFFICER

Wayne Campbell

Although the author has made every effort to ensure that the information in this book was correct at press time and while this publication is designed to provide accurate information in regard to the subject matter covered, the publisher and the author assume no responsibility for errors, inaccuracies, omissions, or any other inconsistencies herein and hereby disclaim any liability to any party for any loss, damage, or disruption caused by errors or omissions, whether such errors or omissions result from negligence, accident, or any other cause.

This publication is meant as a source of valuable information for the reader, however it is not meant as a substitute for direct expert assistance. If such level of assistance is required, the services of a competent professional should be sought. Some information provided is commonly accepted best practice in the security industry or has been proven effective best practice by the author and may not be suitable for certain individuals or enterprises.

Copyright © 2022 Wayne L. Campbell

All rights reserved. No part of this book may be reproduced or used in any manner without the prior written permission of the copyright owner, except for the use of brief quotations in a book review.

To request permissions, contact the author at w.campbell@workmail.com.

Paperback: ISBN 9798799101787

Cover design by Wayne L. Campbell using Gimp 2.10 and Canva

For Chris K. Minamina iā 'oe brah.

Contents

Introduction 1
What is a Security Officer? 3
    Unarmed security officer 4
    Armed security officer 4
    "Tactical" security officer 4
    K-9 security officer 5
Equipment 6
    Uniform 6
    Footwear 10
    Duty belt 12
    Flashlight 15
    Two-way radio 15
    Mobile phone 16
    Handcuffs 16
    Pepper spray 17
    Baton 18
    TASER™ 18
    Firearms 19
Duties 21
    Documentation 22
    Patrol 24
    Static Post 27
    Situational awareness 27
Legal Aspects 30
    Policy and procedure 30

    Liability 31

    Citizen's arrest 31

    Inspections 34

    Judgment 34

    Future, current, and former police officers 35

Organizational Psychology 37

    Customers 37

    Clients 39

    Supervision 40

    Peers 41

    Workplace bullying 42

Security Officer Safety 45

Emergency Response and Management 47

    Preparation 48

    Fire 50

    Civil disturbance 51

    Natural disasters 52

    Bomb threat 52

    Active killer 57

    Power outage 58

Media Management 59

Glossary 60

Bibliography 67

Introduction

This handbook was created to fill the knowledge gap created by expensive textbooks that burden the average entry-level security officer with too much information and cheap ebooks written with good intent but poor execution.

First, most entry-level security officers will have little need for some of the more advanced information in the textbooks, and the cheap ebooks tend to leave out critical entry-level information or flat out give advice that will land the reader in the hospital or in prison.

Secondly, the security profession hasn't enjoyed the best of reputations in recent years, due primarily to poor training and negative media reporting. Many smaller companies don't have the time or the budget to fully train their new hires. While this should never be the case, these companies exist, and they won't be shut down until they commit an offense so egregious that the licensing authority issues sanctions or cancels their license. For those readers that land at one of these companies, tread carefully and consider changing companies quickly.

In my twenty years of working in protective services, I've watched the best and the worst filter through the ranks of both reputable and disreputable companies. The stereotypes of Paul Blart and the snoozing guard are all too common—and yes, they exist—but the bulk of security officers are hard-working individuals committed to ensuring the safety of their clients' properties and the people on site while earning a decent wage.

The intent behind this handbook is to offer a foundation on which to build the new security officer's knowledge. In doing so, I hope to offer the new security officer a reality check on what to expect as a line-level employee in the private security industry.

It should be noted that while much of the information contained in this handbook is suitable for personnel around the globe, the intended primary audience is for security officers employed in the Unites States of America. However, in order to make this handbook useful for the widest possible audience, I will attempt to keep every security officer in mind and will include information for the United Kingdom and Canada.

The phrase **security officer** will be the most frequently used in this book, as the dynamic of the profession has changed from the days of the night watchman and the gate guard.

I make no promises or representations that this field will be suitable for all who pick up this handbook. There will be times when a security officer's perseverance and emotions will be challenged by the people they encounter on the street as well as the people within their own company. These challenges will come daily; the only thing the reader can control is their response (to a degree—even the saintliest among us will lose our temper).

I wish my readers the best of luck in their new endeavor.

-Wayne Campbell

What is a Security Officer?

A **security officer** (or **security guard**) is a person hired to monitor and safeguard property or properties and to ensure the safety of the people who visit or occupy them.

Security officers complete routine patrols to check for security deficiencies, to check for safety hazards, and to make their presence known to criminals. A **foot patrol** is the most common patrol and is completed by walking. A **mobile patrol** is a route completed with the assistance of a vehicle, bicycle, mobility device (e.g. Segway), boat, or other means of conveyance.

Security officers come from many backgrounds, but a large portion are attempting to enter law enforcement careers or have retired from law enforcement. The vast majority are male with a secondary school-level education. Many hold two-year degrees. A few hold university-level degrees. Fewer still hold higher degrees and are generally not found at the line level.

The security officer is not a police officer nor a representative or agent of law enforcement. Security officers are private citizens and have no greater powers of arrest than any other private citizen. The ideal way to think of the security officer is as a *professional witness*.

Security officers are employed generally in one of two designations, (1) proprietary security and (2) contract security.

Proprietary security officers are hired directly as employees by the company for which security services are provided. They may work in a security department or report directly to a designated manager.

Contract security officers are hired by a company that provides security services to a client or several clients on a contractual basis and are not employees of the companies whose location(s) they monitor.

Within these two designations follow four general classifications, detailed below.

Unarmed security officer

An **unarmed security officer** will typically have no self-defense weaponry of any kind, though some companies will still allow rudimentary self-defense weapons like **pepper spray** or a **baton** (sometimes both). This is the most common classification of security officer.

Armed security officer

An **armed security officer** will have any array of self-defense weaponry available, including those mentioned above plus a handgun, shotgun, rifle, or some combination of the three. An armed security officer may also have a **TASER™** as part of their duty gear.

"Tactical" security officer

A new type of niche personnel is the **"tactical" security officer**. The word *tactical* has been placed in quotes here because this classification is normally a sales tool rather than an actual classification. The "tactical" security officer is an armed security officer that maintains a military or SWAT-like appearance.

This is not to say that there aren't special companies that provide special tactical services such as exfil, bodyguard, and executive protection services, but these companies typically run a much more covert operation.

K-9 security officer

The **K-9 security officer** (or **dog section**) is an extension of the "tactical" security officer with the addition of a dog. However, K-9 security officers do add an extra level of deterrence and are useful for search-and-rescue operations or bomb detection at sensitive facilities.

Any of these classifications may be required to obtain a license based on the laws of the jurisdiction in which services are rendered. Be sure to check with the licensing agency(ies) to determine whether a license is required. A good place to start are the webpages below:

United States:
https://www.securityguardtrainingcentral.com/complete-guide-usa-security-guard-license-requirements/

United Kingdom:
https://nationalcareers.service.gov.uk/job-profiles/security-officer

Canada:
https://work.chron.com/security-guard-license-canada-21717.html

Equipment

Uniform

The security officer should have a proper uniform issued by their company that clearly identifies them as a security officer and patches and insignia applied in accordance with applicable law. No legitimate security company will send their personnel into the field without a standard uniform.

The **Class B** uniform is the most frequently issued and most commonly seen uniform as it is the most cost effective and most readily identifiable uniform solution (Figure 1, Figure 1a). Many clients prefer the Class B for its ambiguity at long distances—that is, common criminals will have difficulty determining whether the uniform is worn by a security officer or a police officer.

Where no law exists dictating patches and insignia on a Class B uniform, there should be a minimum of three points of identification (**three points rule**). The company should adhere to the following standard:

- Badge or chest patch on left breast in the style of a badge stating PRIVATE SECURITY or similar, or embroidery plainly reading SECURITY
- Identical patch or emblem on both sleeves with the words PRIVATE SECURITY, SECURITY OFFICER or

SECURITY GUARD plainly visible. Ideally, the patch should also bear the name or acronym of the company

Figure 1: Class B (United States and Canada) uniform. Photo by Kindel Media from Pexels.

Figure 1a: Class B (United Kingdom) uniform with high-visibility vest. Photo by Kindel Media from Pexels.

The **Class A** uniform (Figure 2) is commonly issued at corporate offices, high-rise buildings, casinos, and other venues where the presence of a Class B may be considered too aggressive in appearance for the personnel and visitors. It presents a softer, more businesslike appearance.

Figure 2: Class A uniform. Photo by Allied Universal.

Elements of both Class A and Class B uniforms may be mixed and matched as the company or client choose.

The **Class C** uniform is the least commonly seen in private security and also the most aggressive (Figure 3). It is styled on the Battle Dress Uniform (BDU) created for the military. This uniform is favored by clients who wish to project a paramilitary appearance to protect their assets. In recent years, it has also been adopted by less scrupulous security companies offering "tactical response."

Where no law exists dictating patches and insignia on a Class C uniform, follow the three points rule. The company should adhere to the following standard:

- Badge or chest patch on left breast in the style of a badge stating PRIVATE SECURITY or similar, or embroidery plainly reading SECURITY
- Identical patch or emblem on both sleeves with the words PRIVATE SECURITY, SECURITY OFFICER or SECURITY GUARD plainly visible. Ideally, the patch should also bear the name or acronym of the company
- A large back patch with the word SECURITY plainly visible may be substituted for, or added to, the badge or chest patch

Figure 3: Class C uniform. Photo by Propper.

Regardless of the uniform, it should be clean and pressed prior to reporting to work.
- Sharp creases in the trousers, front and rear of trouser leg
- Sharp creases in shirt sleeves
- Sharp creases in the body of the shirt (Class B and C)
    - One line through the center of each chest pocket
    - Three creases on the back; one from the center of both epaulets and one down the center of the shirt, all equal in distance from one another
        - The shirt may have sewn-in body creases, but the sleeves will still need to be creased while pressing the shirt

A vest may be worn over the uniform, but it MUST be issued by the company and uniform in appearance. If a vest of any kind is worn, ensure that patches and insignia are in line with the three points rule.

If a name tag or name tape is to be worn, it should always be worn on the right side of the chest. If worn on a Class B or Class C uniform, the pocket flap will assist in aligning the name tag/name tape. If worn on a Class A uniform, the name tag should be worn on the right lapel of the jacket. NEVER attach to a Class A shirt unless the backing is magnetic and ONLY if it is allowed by the company or the client.

With the exception of Class C uniforms, ALWAYS keep the shirt tucked in. This serves two functions: it maintains a neat appearance and it keeps the security officer from getting the shirt tail caught in machinery or other hazards present at the job site. When tucking in the shirt, ensure that the button placket aligns with the belt buckle and the fly of the trousers. This is called a **gig line**, and it should form a perfectly straight line down the front of the body.

A Class C uniform is not required to be tucked in if the shirt has four pockets (two on the chest and two near the bottom hem). If a **duty belt** is worn (more on this item later), the edge of the buckle should align with the button placket. If the shirt has two pockets—these will be on the chest—tuck in the shirt and create a straight gig line. ALWAYS wear a belt in the trousers of a Class C uniform.

Footwear

Arguably the most important equipment in the possession of the security officer is a pair of high-quality shoes or boots. The security officer spends most of their time on their feet, and if their footwear is cheaply made, an average eight-hour shift will feel like an eternity.

Footwear should be chosen in accordance with the company's written policy. However, there are style rules that should always be followed:

- Class A
    - If the Class A, or suit, is dark in color (black, navy blue), choose black or dark brown Oxford-style shoes
        - Socks should be dark in color, but feel free to add a little personality

- NEVER wear white socks with a dark suit
  - If the Class A is lighter in color (gray, tan, olive) choose brown Oxford-style shoes
    - Socks should complement the color of the suit, but NEVER white
  - If a belt is worn, it should be leather and it should closely match the color of the shoes
  - If suspenders are worn, they may be any color, but avoid bright or distracting colors and patterns
- Class B
  - Black footwear is acceptable with nearly all colors typically issued (i.e. black, navy blue, coyote/brown, olive drab, dark gray) as all duty accessories will likely be black in color. Ensure the toe box can be easily polished and that the footbed supports all parts of the foot equally
    - Shoes
      - Plain Oxford-style; these offer superior support and cushioning
      - Black cushioned sole socks
    - Boots
      - 6" or 8" shaft (tall part of boot that supports the ankle)
      - Heel no higher than 1½"; any higher will cause heel, calf, and back pain
      - Black cushioned sole socks
- Class C

- Black boots are acceptable for all colors issued, as all duty accessories will likely be black in color
  - 8" or 10" shaft to properly blouse (tuck in) the trousers
  - Blousing bands to properly blouse the trousers; these should have metal hooks or Velcro—do not use rubber bands or hair ties (search YouTube for the method of blousing that works best for you)
    - NEVER wear the trouser leg over the boot like a pair of jeans; this looks slovenly and unprofessional. ALWAYS blouse trousers if issued a Class C uniform

Duty belt

A **duty belt** (Figure 4) may be worn with Class B and Class C uniforms. Even if the security officer is tasked with carrying just a few items, a duty belt is highly recommended. It keeps all issued or approved tools within easy reach and keeps the security officer looking sharp.

Duty belts are generally black or dark brown in color and made of either nylon or leather. They require a **trouser belt** underneath to maintain a stable platform for duty tools. The duty belt attaches to the trouser belt using four to six **belt keepers**. Belt keepers help to keep the duty belt from sliding up and down the body while walking, getting into a patrol vehicle, or sitting in a chair. Belt keepers should always match the color and material of the duty belt.

Figure 4: Leather duty and trouser belt (left), nylon duty and trouser belt (center), leather and nylon keepers (right).

Leather may be plain or patterned; if patterned, the most common pattern is called *basketweave*. Nylon belts also vary in appearance, but not so drastically that it warrants further detail. Whichever platform is chosen, ensure that it aligns with uniform appearance and company policy.

A **light loadout** is generally easier to carry on nylon, and a **heavy loadout** is generally easier to carry on leather. However, in the last 20 years, advances have been made in nylon technologies that make them nearly equal in terms of performance. Leather continues to be far cleaner and neater in appearance, and it is also much easier to clean in dusty or dirty environments. Nylon tends to be more affordable and is easily maintained in urban and suburban environments. Follow the manufacturer's instructions for cleaning (and polishing if choosing leather).

> **Light loadout:** varies by company, but may include phone holster, flashlight, glove pouch, notepad pouch, pepper spray, and handcuffs
>
> **Heavy loadout:** includes light loadout plus baton, handgun, magazines, and/or TASER™

When donning a duty belt, first thread the trouser belt through the belt loops sewn onto the trousers. If the trouser belt has a buckle, ensure to maintain the gig line. Place the duty belt directly on top of the trouser belt, again ensuring to maintain the gig line. Secure the belt in place with the belt keepers. ALWAYS place at least one belt keeper at the rear of the belt as close to the center trouser belt loop as possible. This keeps the belt from riding up when entering a patrol vehicle or sitting in an office chair. The tab edge direction is a preference, but belt keepers placed at the rear of the belt with the tab edge facing downward tend to unsnap when getting into a patrol vehicle or sitting in an office chair.

Setup of the duty belt (Figure 5) will depend on both the wearer's preferences and company policy. An unarmed security officer will have a different loadout than an armed security officer. If operating a patrol vehicle or sitting in a chair for long periods of time, it is advisable to keep most of the loadout toward the front of the belt to reduce back pain. If primarily walking, the loadout should be evenly spaced around the waist to prevent back pain.

Some suggestions for a heavy loadout:
- Flashlight should be either in the middle of the waist on the weak hand side or placed behind the handgun in a way that doesn't interfere with drawing a handgun
- At least two pairs of handcuffs should be available on the belt, and at least one of the two should be accessible by either hand
- Pepper spray should be accessible by either hand
- Baton should be either in the middle of the waist on the weak hand side or placed behind the handgun in a way that doesn't interfere with drawing the handgun
- Magazine pouches should always be worn on the opposite side of the handgun but still easily reachable with both hands

These suggestions should also help when deciding on placement for a light loadout. Again, the duty belt setup is entirely a preference, but ensure that the proper tool can be used with a minimum of thought beforehand.

Figure 5: Example of a proper heavy loadout setup.

Flashlight

The flashlight is the swing shift and graveyard shift security officer's second-most important tool (the first, remember, is footwear). After dark, hazards become difficult to see, and a good flashlight is an absolute must. Be sure to buy a flashlight from a reputable brand. Some useful features will include:

- 200-500 lumens minimum
- Tailcap switch
- Rechargeable
- IP65 or better water resistance rating

Two-way radio

Many security teams still use two-way radios to communicate at their site. Prior to receiving a two-way radio for duty, ensure it has a fresh battery and that it is tuned to the correct channel.

A two-way radio has a delay after pressing the push-to-talk (PTT) button. When using the radio, press the PTT button, pause, then speak. If it's needed, count "one and a two" in your head before speaking, or any variation that allows a one- or two-second delay.

When using a radio in an emergency situation, it will be difficult to remember to do this, so doing it regularly will allow muscle memory to take over.

Lastly, be aware of obstructions that reduce the radio's effectiveness. Buildings covered in stucco and buildings with steel frames act like faraday cages; radio signals will be unreliable if attempting to communicate beyond the walls (inside-out or outside-in).

Mobile phone

A mobile phone is an absolute MUST, especially for security officers in remote locations where they may be the only person on duty. Whether it's a contract plan or a pay-as-you-go plan, EVERY security officer should ALWAYS have a mobile phone in their pocket. If the company doesn't allow personal phones on duty, keep the phone in standby mode and nearby if possible. DO NOT abuse the employer's trust by using the phone when it shouldn't be used.

If the company absolutely will not allow the phone to be in a pocket or nearby, know where the nearest phone is. However, there is no reason for an employer to deny the security officer the ability to call for help.

Like two-way radios, be aware of obstructions that reduce the cellular signal. The security officer will always get better cellular signal outside, even in a dense urban area.

Handcuffs

Handcuffs are a simple tool that provide restraint on combative or hostile subjects, but they are fraught with legalities. If used improperly, they can injure either the subject or the security officer, and just using them can open the security officer to a wide array of civil lawsuits. Of these lawsuits, likely the most frequent is that of false imprisonment, and this is not without merit.

Prior to choosing to carry handcuffs, follow these four simple rules:

- Get proper training and certification from a reputable source even if it is not required by the company or client
- Understand the working parts of the handcuffs chosen
- Know where the key is at all times (keep several spares; there are even belt keepers with hidden keys in the event handcuffs are taken from and used on the security officer)
- DO NOT buy cheap handcuffs, as they WILL fail and endanger both the subject and security officer; buy from a reputable company like Smith & Wesson, Peerless, or ASP

The following equipment is allowable for security officers employed in the United States; nearly all of them are highly restricted or illegal for general public possession and use in the United Kingdom and Canada. *ALWAYS consult governing law(s) PRIOR to carrying ANY weapon on duty.*

Pepper spray

Pepper spray, or **OC spray**, is weaponized *oleoresin capsicum*, the oil extracted from hot peppers that make them hot to the touch (and on the tongue). It is found in stream, fog, foam, and gel varieties. It is a simple and effective self-defense weapon that is easily deployed, but care must be taken when using it. When deploying pepper spray, the user must quickly think about:
- Wind direction
- Number of subjects
- Number of innocent bystanders
- Effective range listed on the packaging or canister

To carry pepper spray while on duty, ensure that company allows it. In many states and provinces, the security officer must have a license. Check with the licensing authority(ies) to determine whether this is the case.

Baton

The baton is a simple but devastating melee weapon. The tip delivers a painful and fight-ending blow to an opponent when used properly. It is such a dangerous weapon that some jurisdictions have outlawed them from being carried by *anyone*.

Prior to choosing to carry a baton, proper training from a reliable and reputable company *is a must*. Carrying a baton must be authorized by the company and allowed under local and state/provincial law.

TASER™

TASER™ systems have been around since the 1970s, but the tools have been facing higher scrutiny in recent years. In general, a TASER™ is an electric weapon that discharges metal probes to deliver incapacitating electrical current to an assailant from a distance of 8-15 feet (2.5-4.5 meters). This weapon is not to be confused with a **stun gun**, which is the electric weapon that must be placed directly on the assailant to deliver electrical current.

Authorizing the carrying of a TASER™ will be entirely up to the company in most jurisdictions, but, as always, check local and state/provincial laws prior to choosing to carry one. Proper training and certification is also highly advised.

However, DO NOT volunteer to be shot by the weapon. If the instructor insists that their students experience the effects of the TASER™, opt for the direct placement (or stun gun) method instead. Many instructors believe being fired upon is a valuable experience in the event of a stray TASER™ probe hitting the security officer or getting tangled in the wires leading to the electrodes[1], even though this occurrence is exceedingly rare.

In the event the student does not wish to experience the effects of a TASER™, a good instructor will respect the student's wishes and move on to another student and will not withhold the certification. If the instructor withholds the certification, immediately report the facility to the proper licensing authority and demand a refund.

Firearms

The sheer volume of weapons and laws prohibit a detailed entry in this handbook. Obviously, the company must authorize their carrying and the local and state/provincial laws must allow it. Carrying a firearm is the single most critical decision the security officer can make. Not only are firearms politically polarizing, but they will invite also invite the attention of some wholly disgusting people. They will taunt the security officer to provoke drawing the firearm, they will throw things such as rocks or bottles at the security officer, some will even attempt to take the firearm while the security officer's back is turned.

A firearm should be carried ONLY as a weapon of defense. It should not leave the holster, vehicle mount, or security cabinet while on duty unless there is an imminent deadly threat to the security officer or innocent citizens. Doing so may open the security

---

[1] AUTHOR'S NOTE: I believe it to be an exercise in stupidity and peer pressure, as most security officers do not make a wage commensurate with the pain and the possibility of losing control of one's bladder and bowels in front of a roomful of trainees; but to each their own.

officer to criminal and civil penalties ranging from fines to imprisonment.

The security officer MUST be THOROUGHLY vetted and trained prior to carrying a firearm on duty, and nearly all jurisdictions require licensure. Aside from normal firearms training, bear in mind:

- NEVER clear a building in which an alarm has sounded. Call the police and OBSERVE while waiting. There is no company or client policy that is worth losing your life
- NEVER use the firearm as a compliance device. This is called *brandishing* and you will go to jail
- NEVER use a firearm as an offensive weapon. This is called *murder* and you will go to jail
- NEVER draw a firearm unless you are absolutely, positively, **1000%** ready to destroy another human being; there is no "shooting to wound" in a life-or-death situation—it's all or nothing

---

FIREARM CONDITION READINESS

Condition 0—Magazine inserted, round in the chamber, safety *off*.
- For Single Action/Double Action (SA/DA) — Hammer is back.

Condition 1—Magazine inserted, round in the chamber, safety *on*.
- For SA/DA—Hammer is back.

Condition 2—Applies to SA/DA primarily. This is a magazine inserted, round in the chamber, hammer forward. For revolvers, it would be rounds inserted into cylinder, cylinder locked into place, hammer forward.

Condition 3—Magazine inserted, no round in the chamber.
- For SA/DA—Hammer is forward.

Condition 4—No magazine inserted, no round in the chamber.
- For SA/DA—Hammer is forward.

Duties

The security officer should be trained to operate above the minimum requirements of the **post**. The post is where the security officer spends the bulk of their time, such as a guard shack where vehicles are stopped prior to entering or exiting a property. There may be many posts at one **site** that require deployment of multiple security officers. A site may be small or may be many acres; it may be a building or a vacant lot. Wherever the site may be or its size, the security officer must be ready to handle any foreseeable situations that may arise.

At every post, there should be a large binder or book called **post orders** (or **post instructions**). These are the instructions provided by the company or client to ensure the security officers assigned to the site can complete their duties. The orders should contain daily routines as well as emergency response protocols for most foreseeable emergencies such as natural disasters, fires, active shooters, bomb threats, etc.

The security officer may be tasked with seemingly unrelated duties as well, which must be completed in addition to their normal duties. Examples of these tasks include:
- Emptying wastepaper bins
- Delivering intraoffice mail
- Minor fence repair

- Light cleaning of workstation
- Light vehicle maintenance, cleaning, and repair
- Light traffic control device maintenance and repair

These tasks may seem trivial or demeaning at first, but they are good opportunities to interact with the property's employees and to build trust. Additionally, these tasks increase the security officer's visibility and is therefore a deterrent to criminal activity.

Documentation

Contrary to Hollywood depictions, the lifeblood of security work—and also police work—is **documentation**. A lot of time will be spent writing, whether it's with pen and paper, on a mobile app, or at a computer.

At most companies, the most common form completed by the security officer is the **Daily Activity Report** (or **DAR**). The DAR is a daily record of all activity completed by the security officer. Think of it as a work journal, with entries made hourly.

Entries should be chronological, and the hour should be noted in **24-hour time format** (commonly called "military time" in the United States).

There should NEVER be a blank spot in the entries, as this could be construed as a sign of laziness or actually sleeping on the job. If nothing of interest occurred during an hour, the entry should look something like:

24-hour format	
0000 = 12:00 AM	1200 = 12:00 PM
0100 = 1:00 AM	1300 = 1:00 PM
0200 = 2:00 AM	1400 = 2:00 PM
0300 = 3:00 AM	1500 = 3:00 PM
0400 = 4:00 AM	1600 = 4:00 PM
0500 = 5:00 AM	1700 = 5:00 PM
0600 = 6:00 AM	1800 = 6:00 PM
0700 = 7:00 AM	1900 = 7:00 PM
0800 = 8:00 AM	2000 = 8:00 PM
0900 = 9:00 AM	2100 = 9:00 PM
1000 = 10:00 AM	2200 = 10:00 PM
1100 = 11:00 AM	2300 = 11:00 PM

0200: *Conducted foot patrol. Nothing of note observed. Patrol completed at 0220.*

The **incident report** is the next most common form completed by the security officer. It is completed at the end of an unusual event that requires special response. Some examples of these events would include assault, battery, fire, earthquakes, and so on.

The security officer should carry a 3"x5" notepad (A7) or similar small notebook that can be carried in the uniform shirt pocket or in a belt pouch. Memory can be faulty and writing down details of a patrol or an incident as they occur will assist in completing the DAR or incident report. If assigned to a site that requires many incident reports, there are special notepads available—called **field interview notebooks**—that have incident, subject (victim, witness, suspect, other), and vehicle portions pre-printed for easy fill-in.

When completing a report of any kind—and even in note-taking—ensure to only write only the facts of what happened. All reports, and your notes, are subject to subpoena and can be used in civil or criminal court proceedings.

While writing, keep in mind the **Four W's**:
- **Who**: any person involved in an incident should be noted
- **What**: what occurred
- **When**: date, time of day, weather conditions, lighting conditions should all be noted
- **Where**: the location(s) at which the incident occurred

If **How**—the unofficial W—is known, it may be included in the report but *only* if witnessed by the security officer. If there are witnesses to an incident, their statements may be taken but shouldn't be included in the body of the incident report. Rather, witness statements should be in a specific section set aside for them or, if such a section doesn't exist, as separate amendments to the report with the report number printed in a corner for cross-reference if the sheets become separated. How should not be speculation, as this may create confusion during investigation and resolution, and may delay necessary changes to the site, policy, or procedure.

Notice that **Why** is missing; the security officer should never try to determine motive, as that is best left to trained police detectives. Motive is difficult to determine under the best of circumstances and requires extensive interviewing that the average security officer (1) does not have time for and (2) is not *trained* to do.

In contract security, some clients will have specific criteria that must be met in the reports, so the security officer should take great care to ensure those criteria are met as long as those criteria do not interfere with the primary criteria of report writing.

The security officer doesn't need to be an English scholar to write a decent report. Basic grammar and spelling are sufficient. Keep these tips in mind:

1. Use common language and avoid law enforcement jargon, (e.g. 10-code, legal terminology).
2. Keep entries as short as possible while including as much information as possible.
3. Avoid using words *you* don't understand.
4. Complete DAR entries as soon as patrols are over
5. Complete incident reports as soon after the incident as possible.
6. Never write anything you don't want seen in court.

The **pass down log** (or **shift change log**) is simply a form or journal in which the security officer leaves important notes for the security officer on the following shift. It may contain company or client requests, directives from supervisors or management, notification of incoming VIPs, or any other notices that will be needed.

Patrol

The two types of patrol, foot and mobile, were introduced in the first chapter. During patrol, the security officer should be checking for common conditions.

1. <u>Broken windows</u> may be the first indicator of a burglary. Inspect the broken window from a distance. If it appears that the glass has been smashed inward (there is no glass or very little glass on the ground outside), a subject may be in the building. Call the police and observe the area while waiting. If an alarm is sounding, call police immediately. If the glass has been smashed outward (most of the glass is on the ground outside), assume the subject is still in the vicinity and call the police. At the end of the incident, complete an incident report.
2. <u>Broken doors</u> are also a likely first indicator of a burglary. DO NOT attempt to clear the building/room. Call the police and observe the area while waiting. At the end of the incident, complete an incident report.
3. <u>Broken locks</u> are not usually identified until a key is inserted. If there is other damage present, especially to the door casing or the door, it may be an indicator of a burglary. Absent this damage, if a broken lock is discovered, contact the assigned person in the post orders. Locks should be fixed quickly. Complete an incident report if required by the post orders. If other damage exists, retreat and request police assistance. At the end of the incident, complete an incident report.
4. <u>Slip hazards</u> (e.g. standing water on the floor, litter in common walkways, oil slicks in driveways and parking lots, etc.). Note the condition of the area and follow the post orders for marking the area and the person(s) to contact.
5. <u>Trip hazards</u> (e.g. upraised concrete slabs on walkways, large obstacles in walkways and parking lots, stakes/grounding rods near walkways, etc.). Note the condition of the area and follow the post orders for marking the area and the person(s) to contact.

6. <u>Loitering</u> is normal around busy shop fronts, but less so around corporate office buildings and office parks. If safe to do so, approach the loiterer and offer assistance. This alerts the person to your presence and they may genuinely need assistance. If the subject refuses, move on and note their movement. Follow post orders for further instructions. NEVER attempt to force a person to leave the site unless they are a danger to themselves and others, and ONLY if there is someone available to assist. If there is no one available to assist, retreat and call police. Afterward, complete an incident report.
7. <u>Littering</u> is a nuisance that nearly all sites must deal with. Note the subject's appearance and their vehicle (if applicable).
8. <u>Suspicious vehicles</u> should be monitored from a distance. If possible, get the license plate FIRST, then note the color, make, and model. Attempt to determine how many occupants are in the vehicle. Even if there is no indication that the occupants may be about to commit a crime, your information could be of use in the future.
9. <u>Suspicious persons</u> should be monitored from a distance. Note their appearance from the bottom up (footwear, pants/skirt, shirt, jacket, hat). After their general appearance has been noted, you may attempt to determine ethnicity, but skin tone is usually a better descriptor (light skin, dark skin) than trying to accurately predict ethnicity. Again, even if there is no indication that the subject may be about to commit a crime, your information could be of use in the future.
10. <u>Fires</u> are easily identified by light and/or smoke. DO NOT attempt to fight a fire on your own. Call **9-1-1 (999)** immediately and report the fire. Attempt evacuation as dictated by post orders.

When completing patrols, try to avoid falling into a routine. This creates predictability, and predictability is an opportunity for criminal conduct. Routine also robs a good security officer of their alertness and allows complacency to take hold, which can lead to the security officer or others getting injured or becoming victims of crime.

Static Post

The **static post** is likely the hardest to work, simply since there is less movement and lends itself to complacency. Luckily, most static posts have some form of foot patrol to complete so the security officer isn't stuck in the same spot for the entire shift. However, there *are* some static posts where the entire shift is spent in one spot. Some examples of these posts are:
- Vehicle gate
- Pedestrian gate
- Lobby security desk
- Entry/exit door

The security officer at these posts will need to get creative in the ways that they keep their minds and bodies alert and limber.

Some suggestions are to do light stretching during downtime and breaks, reviewing the post orders, reviewing

Situational awareness

Whether assigned to a patrol unit or a static post, the security officer must maintain **situational awareness** at all times. The best definition of situational awareness available comes from Great Britain's Health and Safety Executive: "...being aware of what is happening around you in terms of where you are, where you are supposed to be, and whether anyone or anything around you is a threat to your health and safety."

Most security officers work while the rest of their community is asleep, which is to say in the darkness after hours. Because of this, it is imperative that the security officer is alert to their surroundings at all times *without fail*. That is not to say that every security officer is going to be the target of some nefarious criminal element. Rather, it's the mundane that is responsible for many security officer injuries, such as strains, sprains, contusions, abrasions, and lacerations. Inattention to surroundings will lead to slips, trips, falls, and walking into stationary objects.

Another reason to maintain situational awareness is that of **complacency**, or the feeling of quiet pleasure or security while unaware of some potential danger. Security officers have been murdered at their job simply because they weren't paying attention. Complacency may also allow fatigue from long and unusual hours to creep in.

The security officer should always be on the lookout for hostile or suspicious people or circumstances. This is primarily what employers and clients expect of the security officer. If there is any doubt as to what a hostile or suspicious person looks like, consult a supervisor or manager. The security officer should NEVER approach an occupied vehicle from directly behind or directly in front of the vehicle; the occupant may decide to attempt to run over the security officer.

Many contract security companies now offer what are essentially private policing services, with the security officer driving from site to site to conduct patrols of the properties. Security officers assigned this type of vehicle patrol will need to be constantly alert, both for conditions in traffic and environmental conditions at their sites.

While looking for the conditions noted above in the patrol section, the security officer assigned to this vehicle patrol model should also be looking for:
- Road obstacles such as blown tire remnants, items that have fallen out of vehicles (e.g. ladders, boxes, furniture, etc.), and other debris
- Children on foot or riding bicycles/scooters

- Animals
- Speed bumps/humps
- Curbs

Finally, when completing DAR entries or incident reports, make sure to so in a well-lit, controlled location. Controlled means the security officer can see every door, window, and method of approach to their location. If the location is uncontrolled, the security officer is in danger of ambush.

Legal Aspects

The legal side of security work carries far more weight than most new security officers think about. The average entry-level security officer doesn't think of it at all until their first training class, and many don't give it an extra thought until their first incident occurs.

Policy and procedure

Most people believe that policy and procedure are the same thing. However, **policy** is a set of guidelines or rules that determine a course of action. **Procedure** is a series of actions conducted in a certain order or manner. Policies and procedures work in tandem so that every security officer works and responds to their duties in the same way. All security officers must abide by the written policies and procedures contained within the post orders.

Where policies and procedures are absent, and there is a standard way of completing a duty, this is called **standard practice**. Be wary of standard practices; these practices may sometimes run afoul of policy and/or procedure, which opens the security officer and the company to civil or criminal liability. Supervision may sometimes direct the security officer to engage in standard practices, but the security officer should do everything in their power to resist following misguided or plainly dishonest orders.

Liability

Civil liability is a legal obligation that requires a party to pay for damages or to follow other court-enforcements in a lawsuit. This is the most prominent form of liability encountered in the security industry, generally for two (2) reasons.

- Lack of action or negligence in the execution of duties
- Excessive action or restrictions in the execution of duties

As an example, the security officer that writes in their DAR that they were on a foot patrol but they were actually sitting in their vehicle or at the security desk while a woman is raped on the property in proximity to a route that the security officer normally walks could be held civilly liable for the rape.

Foreseeability is a question in contract and tort law that asks how likely it was that a person could have anticipated the potential or actual results of their actions. If a theft occurs in an area where the security officer has documented time and again that a theft could occur, the liability may shift from the security officer to the property owner. However, the security officer may also be liable if they did not document the condition of the area in which the theft occurred while on patrol.

These are just a couple of circumstances that could arise. The security officer should think ahead and, as stated before, write down anything of note while on patrol.

Citizen's arrest

A **citizen's arrest** is an arrest by an ordinary person without a warrant, allowable in certain cases. The security officer *is not obligated* to make a citizen's arrest. Remember, the ideal way to think of the security officer is as a *professional witness*.

Security officers may not arrest or detain subjects under color of law. Certain jurisdictions may allow elevated powers of arrest (such as California and Washington, D.C.), but these security officers must have proper training and credentials denoting these powers.

A security officer <u>may</u> complete a citizen's arrest, as they have no greater authority than that of an ordinary citizen. In California, Penal Code 837 stipulates three (3) conditions under which a private person may arrest another:
- For a public offense committed or attempted in the presence of the citizen
- When the person arrested has committed a felony, although not in the citizen's presence
- When a felony has been, in fact, committed and the citizen has reasonable cause for believing the person arrested to have committed it.

A citizen's arrest is not the same as a **detention**. To detain a person is to hold them against their will in the course of investigation or questioning. Law enforcement may detain a person; security officers <u>may not</u> detain a person except under limited circumstances (e.g. merchant/shopkeeper's privilege).

Further, a citizen is *not* required to comply with a citizen's arrest in the same way that they must comply with arrest by a police officer. A citizen has the moral and ethical duty to respect the reasonable demands of another citizen, but the security officer should be prepared for reasonable demands to either be ridiculed or ignored entirely.

When making the decision to commit to a citizen's arrest, the security officer must weigh several factors quickly and without hesitation:
1. The number of subjects present—are you outnumbered?
2. The subject's demeanor—are they hostile, agitated, calm?
3. The subject's physical fitness—will they be able to outrun or overpower you?

4. The security officer's physical fitness—are you fit enough to effect an arrest if it becomes physical?
5. Weapons present—are there weapons in plain sight or bulges on the subject that suggest a concealed weapon?
6. Escape—are there means and opportunity for escape?
7. Type of offense committed—is the offense an infraction, misdemeanor, or a felony, and is the offense egregious enough to consider arrest?
8. Property owner liability—is it likely the property owner could be sued?
9. Security company liability—is it likely your security company could be sued?
10. Security officer liability—is it likely you could be sued?

This may seem like a long list to try and memorize, but these ten factors will cycle quickly in the mind given proper training and preparation. Even so, there are actions to avoid when attempting a citizen's arrest.

Intimidation is threatening or frightening a person by inducing fear of harm. This is a bully tactic used by novices and unethical security officers. It may also be an arrestable criminal offense in most jurisdictions depending on circumstances and language used.

Most people are familiar with the phrase **excessive force** due to heavy media reporting over the last decade. Excessive force occurs when the force used to make an arrest grossly outweighs the amount of force that is being used by a suspect. Excessive force is universally illegal and opens the security officer to civil and criminal liability.

False arrest occurs when a person is unlawfully detained against their will. For the security officer, false arrest may occur if they did not witness the alleged offense, or if there is no reasonable cause to believe the person committed the offense.

An **illegal search** occurs when the security officer searches a subject to find evidence for making a citizen's arrest. The security officer should only search (or "frisk") a subject for weapons and only if they believe they are in immediate physical danger. The security officer should NEVER conduct ANY search or frisk unless they have been specifically trained to do so.

Inspections

Some facilities require inspection of employee belongings prior to entering or leaving the facility. If required to complete this task, the security officer must remember NEVER to touch the employee or the employee's property. This includes company property assigned to the employee.

> **WHAT'S THE DIFFERENCE?**
>
> **Inspection**: a voluntary examination of belongings or a vehicle to ensure compliance with established policies and procedures.
>
> **Search**: an involuntary examination of a person, their belongings, or their vehicle to discover violations of established policies and procedures.

An inspection is *not* a search and must be conducted with the employee's cooperation. The employer should have notified their employees of the inspection protocol prior to asking security to conduct the inspections. If an employee refuses to cooperate, the security officer should complete a full incident report. Remember, the security officer does not have the right or privilege to conduct a detention.

For contract security officers, clients may sometimes make unreasonable demands for inspections such as opening bags or handling office equipment. The security officer should politely refuse these demands and report the incident immediately to their supervisor. If these demands are made of a supervisor, the supervisor should politely refuse, and the incident should be reported immediately to the account manager or equivalent at the security company.

Judgment

In the exercise of all duties, the security officer should always use their best judgment. Not all security officers will have the same life experience and will act or react in different ways to situations they come across while working. The security officer should always default to what is popularly known as the **Golden Rule**: treat others as you would want to be treated.

There are of course times in which the security officer must take an authoritative role, and no one *wants* to be told what to do; however, even then, the security officer should make their demands respectfully and with proper tone and volume.

When a situation arises that completely takes the security officer by surprise, they should take the same course of action any reasonable person would take. A reasonable person does not run screaming into the night when a fire suddenly breaks out; a reasonable person calls 9-1-1 (999) and ensures the safety of themselves and others while waiting for the fire department.

Luckily, the security officer also has the benefit of having supervisors and management to call—when in doubt, the security officer can and should call supervision for instructions.

Future, current, and former police officers

Those who are in training to be, who are, or who were police officers must suppress the training they've received while working as a security officer. Whereas police training is focused on crime and the enforcement of laws, security training is focused on the safety and security of people and property. Police training is *reactive*, and security training is *proactive*.

Most former police officers have real difficulty accepting this and still apply police thinking and problem-solving to security work; this is fine when conducting preliminary investigation but damaging if the thinking persists into day-to-day work. The police officer working in security must not

- Treat every person encountered as a possible suspect
- Treat their coworkers as inferior

- Treat their supervision as inferior
- Treat the job as inferior

If the former police officer is unable to do this, they should quit immediately and find something more suitable.

Furthermore, former police officers who cannot or will not understand the difference between civil and criminal law are a liability to themselves and others, especially when they learn in a civil court that it only takes 51% certainty (or a "preponderance of evidence") to find them liable for a wrong committed intentionally or negligently while on duty.

For those working in security to gain field experience prior to finishing academy, there is seldom good reason to apply police academy training as a security officer (with a few exceptions, such as report writing and officer safety).

Finally, for police officers who are **moonlighting** in security: be aware that you are still representing your department while on duty. Any action or inaction taken reflects your integrity, the integrity of the hiring company, and the integrity of the police department. Finding yourself on the other side of the table from Internal Affairs and/or the District Attorney for misconduct is going to be *very* uncomfortable and could be the bitter end to a promising career.

Organizational Psychology

This chapter is not an undergraduate or Master's-level summary of a wholly complex field. Rather, it is intended to give the entry-level security officer some simple guidance in navigating the everyday minefield that is working with other people.

Human social constructs are big, complex, and full of free radicals that love to shake up a balanced system. The security officer will be exposed to so many different personalities that attempting to be everything to everyone will be impossible. That is why there are so many standards in place, to ensure that the greatest number of people will—hopefully—receive the exact same courtesies as the people before them.

Customers

A customer is any person who is not a security officer or supervisor with whom the security officer interacts at their job site. They may be a visitor, an employee, or delivery person.

- Never greet a customer while sitting down
- Greet all customers warmly and with a smile
- Always address customers by their preferred title (Mr., Ms., Mrs., Dr., Sir, Ma'am) when appropriate and known

- Use **preferred pronouns** when known (she/her, he/him, they/them)
    - when in doubt, it's okay to ask, "What is your preferred pronoun?" in a polite and respectful manner
    - when in doubt, it's NOT okay to ask, "So, what should I call you?"; this sounds combative and disrespectful
- Eye contact should be made at all times while speaking
- When answering questions, be as brief as possible
- Offer assistance if the customer appears to be at the site for the first time

If a customer becomes irate, the security officer should lower their voice so that the customer is forced to quiet down to hear what the security officer is saying. If the security officer raises their voice, this will agitate the customer and make them louder. Irate customers are not reasonable, so the security officer must be. Once quieted, the security officer can take steps to resolve the issue.

- Don't say "no" or "I can't."
- Offer an alternative
- If the alternative is refused, offer to have them speak with a supervisor
- If speaking with a supervisor is refused, offer to have them speak with a manager
- If all alternatives are refused, offer to take their contact information and have someone get in touch with them at a later time

Some customers, no matter how hard the security officer tries, will be impossible to please. If that becomes the case, the security officer can and should remove themselves from the customer's proximity. If the customer's unreasonable behavior escalates, the security officer should contact police. There should be no warning given; just pick up the phone and dial.

The customer is *not* always right. They may think they are, or believe they are entitled to something to which they are not. Speak calmly, speak clearly, and speak briefly.

Clients

Clients are specific to the contract security industry. A **client** is a company, or a person representing a company, that pays for security services provided by the security officer. They are distinct from customers only by benefit of actually paying the security officer's salary. One way to think of it is: <u>all clients are customers, but not all customers are clients</u>.

Clients may believe that they can ask the security officer to do anything. This is not the case. Clients cannot ask the security officer to do anything in violation of policy, procedure, or law. Further, if a client request makes the security officer uncomfortable, assistance should be sought from supervision.

A good client will make requests of supervision, who will then pass on the request to the security officer. However, there are many bad clients out there who simply do not understand what a security officer may and may not do. It is *not* the security officer's duty to educate the client. Use this phrase when receiving requests or instructions directly from clients:

"*Sure, I'll be happy to do that as soon as I get approval from my supervisor.*"

That's it.

If the client persists, redirect them to supervision. Remember, all clients are customers, so don't so "no" or "I can't." Let someone else do that. The security officer's job is to adhere to policy, procedure, and governing law.

At one point or another, the security officer will get frustrated by a demanding or unreasonable client. None of the above will resolve the situation. In this case, concerns should be shared—calmly—with supervision so that the client can be tamed.

The only time the security officer may say "no" to a client is in the event the client asks the security officer to do something illegal or unethical. At that time, it is absolutely okay to say "no."

Supervision

Supervision are any classification of management tasked with directing the activities of the security officer. Supervisors and managers assist in the day-to-day operations of security services and are responsible for training, scheduling, and client relations.

Ideally, supervision will have risen through the ranks. Supervisors typically will have done so, but managers may not have. More often than not, managers have been hired from the outside so they can bring fresh methods and ideas into an organization. This doesn't mean they're idiots; they may just have a different perspective and will need to be educated on line-level responsibilities.

- Always address supervision by their preferred title (Mr., Ms., Mrs., Dr., Sir, Ma'am) when appropriate and known[2]
    - Use preferred pronouns when known (she/hers, he/his, they/them)

---

[2] AUTHOR'S NOTE: As laughable as it is, if the titles mimic military or police ranking systems, use those, even when you feel stupid saying *Corporal, Sergeant, Lieutenant,* and *Captain*. It feels dumb, it *is* dumb, but it exists. I've even heard of one security company owner who referred to himself as Major General and demanded that he be addressed in that way. Don't let the titles get in the way of treating supervision respectfully.

- when in doubt, it's okay to ask, "What is your preferred pronoun?" in a polite and respectful manner
- when in doubt, it's NOT okay to ask, "So, what should I call you?"; this is combative and disrespectful
- Take direction well; do not argue or press a point unless there is an express consent to speak freely—even then, learn to take "no" for an answer
  - Remember, the security officer is a **subordinate**, regardless of the express or implied consent to speak freely
- When speaking with supervision face-to-face, have a notebook in hand or notepad on the desk; jot down anything of importance—DO NOT doodle

Don't attempt to be friends with supervision; all good security companies frown on **fraternization**, which could land supervision in trouble and make it appear to peers as though the security officer is receiving preferential treatment. Some supervision will look down on the security officer for attempting friendship and treat them poorly afterward. Supervisors and managers are resources, not friends. By all means, be *friendly* and allow idle chat, but refrain from any relationship beyond that of supervision and subordinate. If such a relationship develops, it is wise for one or both to move to positions in which there is no conflict of interest.

Peers

Peers are the people with whom the security officer works every day, and who are likely equal in ability and qualifications. It was stated in the first chapter that security officers come from a variety of backgrounds, including a large portion of those who are attempting to enter law enforcement or who have retired from law enforcement. There are also a significant number of security officers who come from a military background. Frustratingly, these peers may sometimes believe that they are superior because of prior training and skill sets.

Whatever the case may be, security officers all have the same status while on duty—that of a security officer. All security officers at a site must work well together in order to maintain the safety and security of the property and the people who occupy it. Following are some valuable tips for working with your peers.

1. Don't get involved in **war storying** on post; this activity entertains only the person telling it and the stories are mostly untrue anyway. Customers don't want to hear it, and war storying can also be harmful to team morale; some team members will perceive it as arrogance. If war storying is meant to be a bonding experience, it should be done during breaks or social time with like-minded peers away from the job site.
2. Maintain professional distance while at work. Groups of security officers tend to move in cliques, and those cliques tend to hang out off duty; at work, everyone is on equal footing. Everyone should be able to respectfully engage while at work.
    a. While maintaining that professional distance, respect other security officers' **boundaries**, as you expect them to respect yours. Boundaries are psychological limits that protect the integrity of an individual or that helps the person set realistic limits on participation.
3. Don't be confrontational about duties that haven't been completed by another security officer. Take your peer aside and ask them why a task wasn't completed and offer to assist just once. If the behavior is repeated, report it to supervision.
4. Above all, remember the Golden Rule. Simply treat your peers as you would like to be treated at work.

Workplace bullying

Mean and predatory people exist at every level of an organization, whether that organization chooses to recognize it or not. **Bullying,** or the habitual intimidation, abuse, or harassment of another person, is a pervasive threat in the workplace; one that actually can move into the realm of infringing upon a person's civil rights and can be prosecuted as a federal crime. Bullies use their perceived power over others to threaten or coerce a person to comply with their demands.

Threatening a person—showing intent to harm them—is the most commonly understood form of bullying. Playground politics dictated that the biggest and strongest was in charge because they could hurt others. Some people never grow out of this stage of development.

Sometimes the urge to bully develops as time progresses due to consistent imbalances of power that leave an individual feeling bitter and resentful of others.

Coercion is persuading an unwilling person to do something by using threats or force. In many situations, there is a *quid pro quo* provision attached in which supervision threatens a person with losing their job if they don't comply with an order given. Most often this occurs during sexual harassment in the workplace, but it can take other forms. An example of this type of coercion: supervision telling a security officer they will be suspended or fired if they refuse to work an odd shift even though the security officer has previously indicated the shift conflicts with childcare hours. The security officer is then placed in the situation of choosing their child(ren) or their job.

Workplace bullying is nearly always top-down; that is, workplace bullies are normally in supervisory positions. Just remember, when not on duty, supervision has no more control over the security officer than anyone else in their life. It may not feel like it, especially if the security officer is assigned to an on-call position, but they still have the power of "no." Some supervisory bullies will attempt continuing to assert their authority after the shift is over, but the reality is that they're just another person.

The security officer can also be accused of bullying if the aforementioned tactics are used to gain compliance from the people with whom they interact. The security officer, yet again, needs to bear in mind the Golden Rule.

Luckily, even supervision have higher-ups to whom they report. Every employer has policies on harassment, so report the behavior to their direct supervisor. If the workplace bullying doesn't cease, keep pushing it higher and higher until someone listens. In the most extreme cases, that may mean reporting the harasser to law enforcement or regulatory bodies.

Security Officer Safety

Security officer safety was touched on in the chapter "Duties," but it is a high-priority topic that deserves further detail. This short but important chapter will give the security officer valuable tools to stay safe on the job.[3]

1. Be mindful of the job site and its hazards. Situational awareness is key to staying safe on the job. Are there hazardous materials present? Are there falling objects risks? Where are the nearest doors and windows?
2. Wear the issued uniform, and make sure it fits. Fit and form are imperative for the unrestricted movement of limbs. When it's cold outside, wear the issued coat or jacket. If a coat or jacket has not been issued, wear a thick base layer under the uniform shirt.
3. Always carry *authorized* defensive gear. If armed, ensure the firearm is in working order and carried in the condition

---

[3] This list has been adapted from the excellent article "10 Important Tips for Safe and Successful Security Patrol" from El Dorado Insurance Agency, Inc.

authorized by the company and/or client (0, 1, 2, 3, or 4). Whatever gear is carried, ensure it is in a safe and operative state.
4. Conduct patrols at random intervals to reduce predictability.
5. Vary the route taken during patrols to further frustrate criminal activity.
6. While on foot patrol, turn corners carefully and widely to reduce the risk of ambush.
7. Stop, look, and listen! Constant motion creates noise and can cover up the sound of danger approaching. Pausing will allow the security officer to take in greater detail.
8. Maintain a safe distance from subjects during field interviews.
9. Have a base knowledge of all emergency procedures contained within the post orders.
10. Know limitations. The security officer should not respond to any occurrence or incident for which they have not been trained.

Emergency Response and Management

Eventually, all security officers will need to respond to a crisis. Even the slowest of sites will have an issue that will need to be resolved decisively. As in all things, the beginning of resolution is to be prepared. This chapter is meant to be a primer on emergency response, not an all-inclusive guide. Always consult post orders for site-specific response procedures.

First aid, cardiopulmonary resuscitation (CPR), and **automated external defibrillator (AED)** training are highly encouraged for all security officers. If the company doesn't provide it, the security officer should take the courses and get certified on their own. It is valuable training for every day living and will pay for itself with the first life saved.

Of the few benefits of the COVID-19 pandemic, one is that many organizations now offer fully-online training that allows security officers to take the training at their leisure, which is of great value to security officers assigned to swing and graveyard shifts.

- As of publication, the most comprehensive and affordable training available in the U.S. is the Adult, Child and Baby First Aid/CPR/AED online class given by the Red Cross

    https://www.redcross.org/take-a-class/classes/adult-child-and-baby-first-

aid%2Fcpr%2Faed-online/a6R3o000001vv3D.html.
- For those in the U.K., a First Aid in the Workplace certification is available from PD Training https://pd-training.co.uk/product/first-aid-in-the-workplace/.
- Canadian residents can earn a Level C equivalent from SimpleCPR for a fraction of the price of more costly blended courses elsewhere https://www.simplecpr.com/adult-child-infant-cpr-first-aid.

Preparation

Before the security officer can respond to any emergency, they must know their site(s) intimately.

- Have a quick reference list of all emergency phone numbers with the contact person/organization clearly labeled
    - If issued a site mobile phone, ensure those numbers are programmed into the phone
- Know the location of all emergency exits
- Know the location of all fire extinguishers
- Know the location of first aid kits and AEDs
    - Ensure first aid kits are always fully stocked
    - Change batteries in AEDs according to manufacturer recommendations (usually every 2-5 years)
    - Change shock pads on AEDs according to manufacturer recommendations (usually every 2-4 years)
- Know the location of utility shutoffs (electrical, water, and gas)
- Know the location of emergency key boxes for police and fire department personnel

- Ask the company to maintain emergency two-way radios
  - If rechargeable, ensure the radio is always in the charging dock and ready to deploy
  - If not rechargeable, keep batteries out of the radio but nearby so they may be inserted quickly; rotate the batteries every 6-12 months
  - Test the radios monthly to ensure they are working and in good repair
  - If the company cannot or will not supply them, ensure your personal mobile phone is at least 80% charged at all times
- Ensure flashlights are working properly at all times
  - If used heavily, ensure batteries are changed every month
  - Consider keeping spare flashlights and light sticks at the site; as with radios, rotate the flashlight batteries every 6-12 months
- Consider keeping a radio at the site with the ability to receive emergency broadcasts; many have hand cranks that make it unnecessary to have batteries on hand
  - Test the radio monthly to ensure the battery or capacitor will hold a charge in the event of an actual emergency
  - If battery-operated, rotate the batteries every 6-12 months
- Keep emergency water rations and rotate the stock a minimum of once per year

The security officer should also keep a 72-hour supply of any regularly taken prescriptions and over-the-counter medications with them. The security officer should also consider a 72-hour supply of emergency food on hand. An emergency can happen at any time, and the security officer should be prepared to be stuck at the site.[4]

Fire

- Smoke is usually the first indicator of a fire. The color of the smoke may indicate what is on fire.
    - White: could mean the fire is just starting, or light, easily combustible fuels such as grass or sticks are on fire
    - Black: heavy fuels that are not easily burned; may also indicate manmade objects are on fire
    - Gray: may indicate that the fire is slowing down and running out of fuels
- Report smoke immediately and broadcast your position
    - If on post alone, call the dispatch center or supervision
- Investigate only briefly; if a source can't be identified, notify the fire department
- If a fire is found, DO NOT ATTEMPT TO FIGHT THE FIRE BY YOURSELF. Seal off the area and call 9-1-1 (999).
- Retreat to a safe location
- If the site is occupied, follow site evacuation procedures.

---

[4] AUTHOR'S NOTE: I'm going to tell you what no other handbook or manual will say: your life is worth more than any property. If the site is unoccupied, you are under no obligation to trade your life for someone else's property. However, if there are people at your site that depend on you to provide life-saving assistance, you should do everything in your power to help.

- If the site is occupied, stay as far away from the fire as possible and document everything in your notebook
  - If there is low or no light, use the notes feature on your mobile phone
- After the fire is contained, follow all instructions from the fire department
- Stay on post until properly relieved or until the company or client releases you from duty

Civil disturbance

More than ever, civil disturbances are disrupting the way people live. Demonstrations, strikes, and riots are becoming more commonplace as people become dissatisfied to slights and wrongs, whether real or imagined.

Regardless of the cause of a civil disturbance, the average security officer should refrain from ever getting involved in any way. There are special teams that exist who are trained and prepared to handle these kinds of events, and most of the time they are sworn law enforcement.

- If the event is peaceful, organized, and on the property, the security officer MAY ask the leader—or the person who appears to be the leader—to relocate. If they do not comply, call the police *non-emergency* number to report the incident
- If the event is NOT peaceful or organized, and it is on the property, contact supervision and initiate lockdown procedures in the post orders prior to calling 9-1-1 (999)
- Take extensive notes of what is occurring for entry into an incident report
- Be on the lookout for agitators and instigators who are trying to turn peaceful events into riots

- Remain on post until the all-clear is given by the police and you are properly relieved or released by the company or client
  - It may not be safe to depart even after you are relieved/released; attempt to determine the safest route away from the site prior to leaving—if unsafe conditions persist, stay as long as is necessary to evade danger

Natural disasters

A **natural disaster** can happen at any time, anywhere, with or without prior notice.
- Ensure your safety and that of others
- Retreat to the safest possible location
- Turn on your emergency radio and listen for updates
- Remain on post until the end of the event if practical and safe to do so; if it is not practical or safe, evacuate
- Follow all instructions given by any emergency services personnel that arrive

Eventually, the disaster will end. Know all procedures in the post orders listed for the particular natural disaster that may occur at the property.

Bomb threat

Bomb threats are not as prevalent today as they were in the last 30 years of the 20th century, but they are still an emergency to be anticipated. A bomb threat may be phoned in, or someone may leave a suspicious package on or near the property. In the most extreme example, a suspect may wear a vest or backpack wired with explosives or dummy explosives.

If the bomb threat is called in, use a checklist similar to the one on the next page to get as much information as possible about the bomb and the caller.

BOMB THREAT PROCEDURES

This quick reference checklist is designed to help employees and decision makers of commercial facilities, schools, etc. respond to a bomb threat in an orderly and controlled manner with the first responders and other stakeholders.

Most bomb threats are received by phone. Bomb threats are serious until proven otherwise. Act quickly, but remain calm and obtain information with the checklist on the reverse of this card.

If a bomb threat is received by phone:

1. Remain calm. Keep the caller on the line for as long as possible. DO NOT HANG UP, even if the caller does.
2. Listen carefully. Be polite and show interest.
3. Try to keep the caller talking to learn more information.
4. If possible, write a note to a colleague to call the authorities or, as soon as the caller hangs up, immediately notify them yourself.
5. If your phone has a display, copy the number and/or letters on the window display.
6. Complete the Bomb Threat Checklist immediately. Write down as much detail as you can remember. Try to get exact words.
7. Immediately upon termination of call, DO NOT HANG UP, but from a different phone, contact authorities immediately with information and await instructions.

If a bomb threat is received by handwritten note:

- Call _____
- Handle note as minimally as possible.

If a bomb threat is received by e-mail:

- Call _____
- Do not delete the message

Signs of a suspicious package:

- No return address
- Excessive postage
- Stains
- Strange odor
- Strange sounds
- Unexpected delivery
- Poorly handwritten
- Misspelled words
- Incorrect titles
- Foreign postage
- Restrictive notes

* Refer to your local bomb threat emergency response plan for evacuation criteria

DO NOT:

- Use two-way radios or cellular phone. Radio signals have the potential to detonate a bomb.
- Touch or move a suspicious package.

WHO TO CONTACT (Select One)
- 911
- Follow your local guidelines

For more information about this form contact the Office for Bombing Prevention at: OBP@cisa.dhs.gov

BOMB THREAT CHECKLIST

DATE: _____ TIME: _____

TIME CALLER HUNG UP: _____   PHONE NUMBER WHERE CALL RECEIVED: _____

Ask Caller:

- Where is the bomb located? (building, floor, room, etc.)
- When will it go off?
- What does it look like?
- What kind of bomb is it?
- What will make it explode?
- Did you place the bomb? Yes No
- Why?
- What is your name?

Exact Words of Threat:

_____
_____
_____

Information About Caller:

- Where is the caller located? (background/level of noise)
- Estimated age:
- Is voice familiar? If so, who does it sound like?
- Other points:

Caller's Voice	Background Sounds	Threat Language
☐ Female	☐ Animal noises	☐ Incoherent
☐ Male	☐ House noises	☐ Message read
☐ Accent	☐ Kitchen noises	☐ Taped message
☐ Angry	☐ Street noises	☐ Irrational
☐ Calm	☐ Booth	☐ Profane
☐ Clearing throat	☐ PA system	☐ Well-spoken
☐ Coughing	☐ Conversation	
☐ Cracking Voice	☐ Music	
☐ Crying	☐ Motor	
☐ Deep	☐ Clear	
☐ Deep breathing	☐ Static	
☐ Disguised	☐ Office machinery	
☐ Distinct	☐ Factory machinery	
☐ Excited	☐ Local	
☐ Laughter	☐ Long distance	
☐ Lisp		
☐ Loud		Other Information:
☐ Nasal		
☐ Normal		
☐ Ragged		_____
☐ Rapid		
☐ Raspy		_____
☐ Slow		
☐ Slurred		_____
☐ Soft		
☐ Stutter		_____

Figure 6: Dept. of Homeland Security bomb threat checklist, adapted for the Cybersecurity & Infrastructure Security Agency.

There may be a time when the security is tasked to be a member of a bomb search team. The security officer should only accept if (1) they are comfortable doing so, and (2) if they know the property well enough to *actually* be of help. The following figures show common procedures for a bomb sweep. NEVER sweep for a bomb alone; ALWAYS sweep with another security officer, police officer, or other trained person(s).

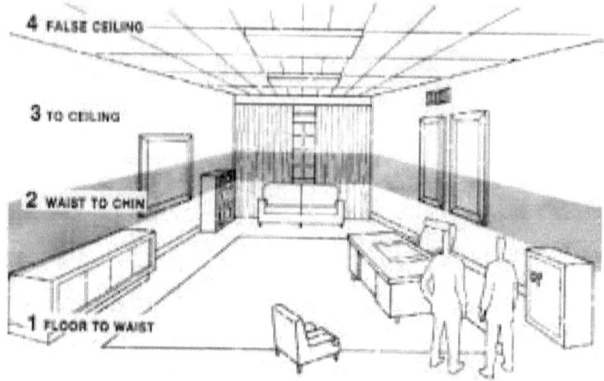

Figure 7: Levels of a bomb search—divide the room by height and search from floor to ceiling.

Figure 8: Search the area by height and assigned position, overlapping if necessary.

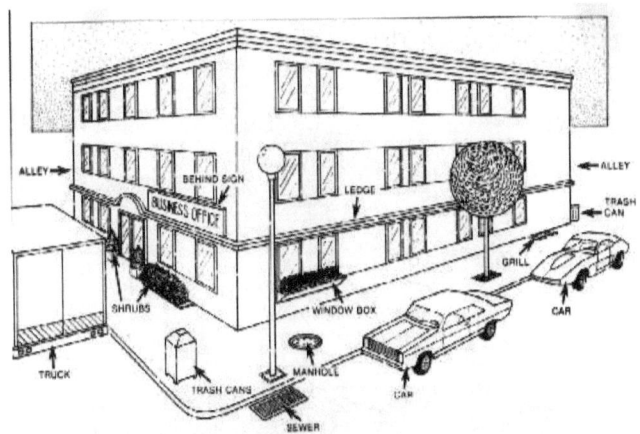

Figure 9: Exterior search areas.

If anything suspicious is found, DO NOT TOUCH IT, AND DO NOT USE A MOBILE PHONE OR TWO-WAY RADIO NEAR IT. Leave it where it is and retreat from the area.

Many bombs in history have had a **mercury switch** that arms and/or detonates a bomb when it is moved. Others have had pressure switches that detect when the sides of a container are compressed. Still others have been activated by mobile phones or radio signals. So, again, the absolute rule here is: **DO NOT TOUCH IT, AND DO NOT USE A MOBILE PHONE OR TWO-WAY RADIO NEAR IT.**

Some examples of suspicious objects follow on the next page in Figures 10-12.

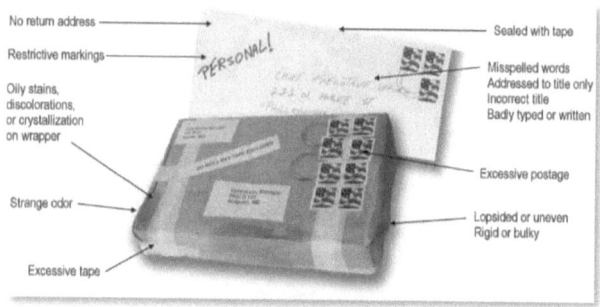

Figure 10: Suspicious envelopes and packages.

Figure 11: Boxes with unknown contents and items poking out the sides and/or corners.

Figure 12: Luggage, duffel bags, or backpacks left unattended near structural elements of a building or near crowds.

Active killer

Active killer events have been increasing in the last 20 years, culminating in one of the deadliest mass shooter incidents in history on October 1, 2017 in Las Vegas, Nevada; the shooter killed 60 people and wounded 411. In total, there were nearly 1,000 casualties by the end of the incident.

However, there have been incidents involving other weapons, hence why this type of incident has evolved from the active *shooter* to the active *killer* event. For instance, in the same year as the Las Vegas shooting, zealots drove a van onto London Bridge and used it to run over people before disembarking the vehicle and beginning a stabbing campaign. It was one of three seemingly related attacks that year in England, the deadliest being a suicide bombing at Manchester arena. In Canada, a mentally ill man, the son of the local police inspector, stabbed five people to death at a university party.

Active killer incidents occur seemingly out of the blue, progress quickly, and generally end abruptly. The security officer, and all others in the vicinity, need to act quickly and decisively to save their life and the lives of others.

RUN. The first thing to do is to get away from the active killer. Escape and evasion is the safest course of action.

HIDE. If escape and evasion aren't possible, find cover or concealment. When available, take refuge in a room with doors and windows that can be locked. Turn off the lights. Silence mobile phones and radios.

U.S. and Canada—FIGHT. As a last resort, and only if the security officer's life or the life of others is in danger, fight back. Use anything available; chairs, fire extinguishers, binders, anything hard and unyielding. Use pepper spray or baton if available. If armed, fire at will, remembering to know what's behind your target and maintaining controlled fire.

UK—TELL. When the security officer has found a safe location, dial 999 and give as much detail as possible.

Power outage

A power outage my occur on its own or concurrently with any of the emergencies covered previously.

- Notify supervision
- Contact the electrical utility provider as directed by the post orders and supervision
- Keep people calm and assist in evacuation as directed by the post orders
    - If at a remote or unoccupied post, engage protocols as dictated by the post orders
    - If no evacuation is necessary, maintain order on post and be a calm presence for other occupants
- Maintain contact with other security officers and supervision
- Request regular updates from the electrical utility provider
- If there are generators or uninterrupted power supply (UPS) battery banks on site, continually check the health of the system and forward updates to supervision or the designated systems maintenance contact
- Remain on post until properly relieved or released by the company or client

Media Management

After an incident has concluded, there will likely be members of the media present pushing for interviews. This will be the shortest chapter, as there are only three things to remember:
1. Direct all media personnel to the company or client media contact
2. Say nothing about the incident
3. Repeat 1 and 2

Glossary

24-hour time format—standard time; also called "military time" in the United States.

9-1-1—emergency number used to contact police, fire departments, and emergency medical services in North America.

999— emergency number used to contact police, fire departments, and emergency medical services in the United Kingdom.

Armed security officer—A security officer authorized to carry self-defense weaponry including deadly weapons (handgun, shotgun, rifle).

Automated external defibrillator (AED)—device used to analyze a person's heart rate and rhythm, and to shock it into functioning normally during a cardiac event.

Baton—A stick-like weapon that may be a solid rod or collapsible. Solid batons are generally made of wood, collapsible batons are generally made of metal.

Belt keepers—Strips of leather or nylon wrapped around both the duty belt and trouser belt to keep the duty belt in a fixed position on the waist.

Boundaries (physical security)—invisible lines that define the limits or end of a property.

Boundaries (professional distance)—psychological limits that protect the integrity of an individual or that helps the person set realistic limits on participation.

Bullying—the habitual intimidation, abuse, or harassment of another person.

Cardiopulmonary resuscitation (CPR)—emergency respiration procedure for victims experiencing a medical emergency.

Citizen's arrest—an arrest by an ordinary person without a warrant, allowable in certain cases.

Civil disturbance—acts of disorder that disrupt public law and order, such as demonstrations, strikes, and riots.

Class A Uniform—A uniform consisting of a suit jacket, suit trousers, dress shirt, and dress shoes. May or may not include a tie.

Class B Uniform—A uniform consisting of a pressed shirt, pressed trousers (my have low-profile cargo pockets), and Oxford-style shoes or tactical boots. May or may not include a tie.

Class C Uniform—A uniform consisting of a pressed cargo shirt with two or four pockets, cargo pants, and tactical boots. Modeled after military uniforms.

Client— a company, or a person representing a company, that pays for security services provided by the security officer.

Coercion—persuading an unwilling person to do something by using threats or force.

Complacency—the feeling of quiet pleasure or security while unaware of some potential danger.

Contract security—Security services provided by a company which hires security personnel and places them at client sites.

Customer—any person who is not a security officer or supervisor with whom the security officer interacts at their job site.

Daily Activity Report (DAR)—A daily record of all activity completed by the security officer.

Detention—to detain a person is to hold them against their will in the course of investigation or questioning.

Documentation—any written record in any format, including paper (hard copy), electronic (soft copy), audio recordings, and video recordings.

Duty belt—A belt worn to carry tools and weaponry.

Excessive force—force used to make an arrest that grossly outweighs the amount of force that is being used by a suspect.

False arrest—when a person is unlawfully detained against their will.

Field interview notebook—a pre-printed notebook that has incident, subject (victim, witness, suspect, other), and vehicle portions pre-printed for easy fill-in.

Firearm—Any weapon (including a starter gun) which will or is designed to or may readily be converted to expel a projectile by the action of an explosive (Bureau of Alcohol, Tobacco, Firearms and Explosives)

First aid—immediate emergency medical treatment of minor to serious illness or injury to preserve life until regular medical attention can be given.

Foot patrol—A routine patrol completed by walking.

Foreseeability—a question in contract and tort law that asks how likely it was that a person could have anticipated the potential or actual results of their actions.

Four W's—Who, What, When, Where; Why points to motive, shouldn't be included in a factual report. How may be entered in a report ONLY if witnessed by the security officer.

Fraternization—the act of supervision associating with a subordinate outside of the work environment.

Gig line—A perfectly straight line along the body created by aligning the shirt placket, belt buckle edge, and trouser fly.

Golden Rule—treat others as you would want to be treated.

Heavy loadout—includes light loadout plus baton, handgun, magazines, and/or TASER™

Illegal search—when the security officer searches a subject to find evidence for making a citizen's arrest.

Incident report—A form completed at the end of an unusual event that requires special response (e.g. fire, earthquake, assault, battery, etc.)

Inspection—a voluntary examination of belongings or a vehicle to ensure compliance with established policies and procedures.

Intimidation— threatening or frightening a person by inducing fear of harm.

K-9 security officer—A "tactical" security officer with the addition of a dog.

Light loadout—varies by company, but may include phone holster, flashlight, glove pouch, notepad pouch, pepper spray, and handcuffs

Mercury switch—an electrical switch that opens and closes a circuit when a small amount of the liquid metal mercury connects metal electrodes to close the circuit.

Military time—see **24-hour time format**.

Mobile patrol—A routine patrol completed with the assistance of a vehicle, bicycle, mobility device (e.g. Segway), boat, or other means of conveyance.

Moonlighting—having a second job in addition to one's regular employment; may or may not be related to the primary job.

Natural disaster—event such as an earthquake, severe weather, flood, or wildfire

OC spray—see **Pepper spray**

Pass down log (or shift change log)—a form or journal in which the security officer leaves important notes for the security officer on the following shift.

Peers—the people with whom the security officer works every day, and who are likely equal in ability and qualifications.

Pepper spray—Weaponized pepper in an aerosol form containing the extract oleoresin capsicum, the oil that makes pepper hot to the touch; may be found in stream, fog, foam, or gel varieties.

Policy— a set of guidelines or rules that determine a course of action.

Post instructions—see **post orders**.

Post orders—A book or binder of instructions provided by the company or client to ensure the security officers assigned to the site can complete their duties.

Post—Where a security officer spends the bulk of their time, such as a guard shack where vehicles are stopped prior to entering or exiting a property.

Preferred pronoun—the pronoun that a person prefers to be used when they are referred to, in order to indicate their gender identity.

Procedure—a series of actions conducted in a certain order or manner.

Proprietary security—Security services provided by personnel hired directly by the company at which they work.

Search—an involuntary examination of a person, their belongings, or their vehicle to discover violations of established policies and procedures.

Security officer (or **security guard**)—A person hired to monitor and safeguard property or properties and to ensure the safety of the people who visit or occupy them.

Shift change log—see **pass down log**.

Site—The property at which a security officer is posted or employed.

Situational awareness—being aware of what is happening around you in terms of where you are, where you are supposed to be, and whether anyone or anything around you is a threat to your health and safety.

Standard practice—a way of doing things not covered by policy or procedure, typically undocumented.

Stun gun—A handheld electrical weapon that delivers an incapacitating electrical current directly to an assailant's body. Not to be confused with TASER™.

Subordinate—a person holding a lower rank or social position.

Supervision—any classification of management tasked with directing the activities of the security officer.

"Tactical" security officer—An armed security officer with a military or SWAT-like appearance.

TASER™—An electric weapon that discharges metal probes to deliver incapacitating electrical current to an assailant from a distance of 8-15 feet (2.5-4.5 meters). Not to be confused with Stun gun.

Threatening—showing intention of bodily harm.

Three points rule—A standard dictating there should be a minimum of three points of identification on a security officer's uniform, such as sleeve patches and a chest badge.

Trouser belt—A belt worn to hold up trousers and to provide a stable base for a duty belt.

Unarmed security officer—A security officer not authorized to carry self-defense weaponry.

War storying—telling stories of past experiences or exploits, usually exaggerated for dramatic effect.

Bibliography

Bureau of Security and Investigative Services. "Power to Arrest Training Manual." Bureau of Security and Investigative Services, last modified June 2015.
https://www.bsis.ca.gov/forms_pubs/poa.pdf

Department of Homeland Security. "Department of Homeland Security Bomb Threat Checklist." Cybersecurity & Infrastructure Security Agency, v2 n.d. Accessed January 7, 2022.
https://www.cisa.gov/sites/default/files/publications/Bomb-Threat-Procedure-Checklist.pdf

El Dorado Insurance Agency, Inc. "Safe and Successful Security Patrol: 10 Practical Tips." El Dorado Insurance Agency, Inc., May 22, 2020. Accessed January 5, 2022.
https://www.eldoradoinsurance.com/el-dorado-news/10-important-tips-safe-successful-security-patrol/

Halek, G. "Firearm Condition Readiness: Condition 0, Condition 1, Condition 2, Condition 3, Condition 4 -- What Do They All Mean?" Concealed Nation, August 31, 2015. Accessed January 5, 2022. https://concealednation.org/2015/08/firearm-condition-readiness-condition-0-condition-1-condition-2-condition-3-condition-4-what-do-they-all-mean/

Health and Safety Executive. "Knowing what is going on around you (situational awareness)." Health and Safety Executive, last modified June 2012.
https://www.hse.gov.uk/construction/lwit/assets/downloads/situational-awareness.pdf

Roach, D.W. *21st Century Security Officer: Career Guide*. Helsinki: Creativia, 2018.

Security Guard Training Central. "The Complete Guide to USA Security Guard License Requirements." Security Guard Training Central. Accessed December 29, 2021.
https://www.securityguardtrainingcentral.com/complete-guide-usa-security-guard-license-requirements/

Strom, Kevin, Marcus Berzofsky, Bonnie Shook-Sa, Kelle Barrick, Crystal Daye, Nicole Horstmann, and Susan Kinsey. "The Private Security Industry: A Review of the Definitions, Available Data Sources, and Paths Moving Forward." RTI International, December 2010.
https://www.ojp.gov/pdffiles1/bjs/grants/232781.pdf

Universal Protection Service. "Security Training Module Series." Universal Protection Service, UPS University ©, Modules 1-26, n.d.

Universal Protection Service. *Emergency Response Guide for Security Personnel*. Universal Services of America. Santa Ana: Corporate Offices, 2010.

Workplacebullying.org. Workplace Bullying Institute. Accessed January 5, 2022. https://workplacebullying.org

Zippia, Inc. "Security Guard Statistics and Facts in the U.S." Zippia, Inc. Accessed December 29, 2021. https://www.zippia.com/security-guard-jobs/demographics/

www.ingramcontent.com/pod-product-compliance
Lightning Source LLC
Chambersburg PA
CBHW031536210526
45464CB00003B/1043